TERRORIST ATTACKS

THE NERVE GAS ATTACK ON THE TOKYO SUBWAY

J. Poolos

The Rosen Publishing Group, Inc.
New York

Published in 2003 by The Rosen Publishing Group, Inc.
29 East 21st Street, New York, NY 10010

Library of Congress Cataloging-in-Publication Data

Poolos, J.
The nerve gas attack on the Tokyo subway / by J. Poolos. — 1st ed.
    p. cm. — (Terrorist attacks)
Includes bibliographical references and index.
ISBN 0-8239-3653-8 (lib. bdg.)
1. Oumu Shinrikyåo (Religious organization) 2. Terrorism—Religious aspects—Oumu Shinrikyåo (Religious organization) 3. Terrorism—Japan.
I. Title. II. Series.
BP605.O88 P66 2002
364.15'23'0952—dc21

                                                  2001007610

CONTENTS

INTRODUCTION

At first glance, the terrorist attacks on the World Trade Center and the Pentagon on September 11, 2001, seem to have little in common with the release of sarin, a deadly nerve gas, into the Tokyo subway system in March 1995. The September 2001 attacks were a series of well-choreographed strikes in our own backyard that claimed the lives of thousands. The sarin attack occurred halfway around the world and resulted in fewer than fifteen deaths. Yet the attacks share at least one major characteristic: Both were acts of terrorism.

The attacks in New York and Washington, D.C., were directed at innocent civilians, as was the attack in Tokyo. Both were exquisitely mapped out to the last detail, the result of months and even years of planning and research. Both involved unconventional and extreme means of delivery, not to mention extreme risk. Not only would the lives of the terrorists be risked and in some cases sacrificed, but each act would require both precision and luck to succeed.

Smoke rises from the site of the World Trade Center a few days after the September 11, 2001, terrorist attacks that killed more than 3,000 people in New York City and Washington, D.C.

But the most haunting parallel of those mornings, six years apart, is that the attacks were each the result of powerful visions of disgruntled individuals. These individuals possessed both the charisma and the power to convince large numbers of followers of the importance of a common cause: to disrupt the flow of life as the world knows it.

History has proven that acts of terrorism are born of political groups seeking radical change. It can be said that all terrorist acts are conceived and executed for one of two reasons: to accomplish a specific goal or to get a general response. Modern instances of terrorism have borne this out. For example, during the 1972 Olympics in Munich,

Germany, members of a group called Black September took hostage and later killed Israeli athletes. Black September was demanding the release of 200 imprisoned Palestinian terrorists. This is an example of a terrorist act where a political party used hostages as leverage. The specific goal was to force the release of the Palestinian prisoners.

An example of a terrorist act used to evoke a general response is the bombing of the Alfred P. Murrah Federal Building in Oklahoma City in 1995. This blunt attack on the federal government instilled a severe paranoia in a nation that had previously thought itself immune to such violence. The Oklahoma City bombing showed us what terrorism could do to a nation. Terrorists want to unsettle citizens, to cause them to question the competency of their leadership. They want to turn a population against its government.

The gas attack on Tokyo fits this model like a glove. Its leader, Shoko Asahara, was a social outcast with a criminal record. Asahara had the ability to convince well-meaning people to devote their lives and finances to his cause. His commitment to a singular vision outweighed any reasonable notion of common sense. He possessed the means to carefully plan an act of terror that would require precise timing and faithful execution. And he was motivated by the prospect of bringing a nation to its knees.

But what makes the Tokyo gas attack unique among terrorist acts is the fact that it revolved not around a political movement, or even a religion. The center was a so-called doomsday cult in Japan, the most economically stable, prosperous, and peaceful major nation in the world at the time. How was the neat, orderly population of Tokyo to react to such an inconceivable insult to its very makeup? Even today the effects of the attack linger, particularly with those who were exposed to the gas. A progressive, upwardly mobile world center, Tokyo suddenly found itself doubting its future. The city was paralyzed by the sense of insecurity that can overwhelm a people just after they are brutally blindsided.

Established in 1987 by Shoko Asahara, who is seen here ministering to his followers, Aum Shinrikyo aimed to destroy the world. Asahara believed he was superhuman and would survive Armageddon.

AUM SHINRIKYO, THE SUPREME TRUTH

During Japan's progressive rise to prominence and strength in the world economy, instances of hard work, honor, and achievement dominated the headlines. At the same time, incidents involving a radical cult began to surface.

In 1989, Tsutsumi Sakamoto, a well-respected attorney, was approached by a family trying to locate their child. He was told the youth had been brainwashed and was now enslaved to a charismatic con man. Sakamoto accepted the case and took conventional measures to establish a legal means for gaining custody of the child. Five months later, Sakamoto, along with his wife and infant son, disappeared mysteriously. The case was never solved.

In early February 1995, sixty-eight-year-old notary public Kiyoshi Kariya was distraught to hear that his sister was turning over ownership of the building that housed his office to the very same con man. The sister soon disappeared without a trace. On February 28, Kariya himself was abducted. According to witnesses, he was stopped by several men who then pulled him into a van. Kariya was never seen again. Shortly thereafter, a similar van was found with traces of his blood and the fingerprints of several known members of the cult led by the charismatic con man.

The cult was Aum Shinrikyo, the cult of the Supreme Truth. Its members were devoted to a powerful outcast named Shoko Asahara. Asahara claimed that those who believed in his teachings and writings would achieve enlightenment and feats like levitation. The abductions of members and their relatives were the first of several incidents to preface an act of terrorism that would have far-reaching effects on Japan's psyche.

Shoko Asahara's Beginnings

According to journalist Shoko Egawa, Shoko Asahara was born Chizuo Matsumoto in 1955 on Kyushu, one of Japan's main islands. He was sightless in one eye and partially blind in the other at birth. This disability was to prove a significant factor in Asahara's behavior and his evolution into the leader of one of the world's most recognizable cults.

At the age of six, Asahara was sent to a school for the blind in the city of Kumamoto, which his brother also attended. Students at the school remember young Asahara as a manipulative bully who used the advantage of his partial sight to lord over the rest of the kids, who were totally blind. A former teacher recalls that Asahara once threatened to burn down a dormitory. When confronted, he denied ever making such threats. He forced other students to give him

Shoko Asahara was born in 1955 on Kyushu, one of Japan's main islands. His given name was Chizuo Matsumoto. After a visit to India in 1986, he changed it to what he thought was the holier name of Shoko Asahara.

money in exchange for protection. He also boasted that one day he would become prime minister of Japan. Based on these recollections, it's no surprise that he repeatedly failed to win class office in student elections.

After graduating, Asahara opened a pharmacy specializing in traditional Chinese medicines. He made a quiet living until 1982, when he was arrested for selling fake cures. Devastated by a bankrupt business and a reputation in ruins, he lived in isolation. But by 1984 the "future savior" began to refine his dream of redemption and founded a school for yoga. It was a great success, and Asahara enjoyed the reputation of a respected teacher. Yet already the signs of the megalomania that would characterize his role as leader of Aum Shinrikyo were beginning to show.

Perfect Timing

Japan's booming economy in the 1970s and 1980s spurred many so-called new religions, which offered spiritual refuge to young people who didn't know what to make of materialism. Shoko Asahara was in stride with the trend. He embarked on a Himalayan retreat, returning to boast of having achieved his *satori*, a Japanese term for enlightenment. This, he claimed, was triggered by his first success at self-levitation. Asahara felt empowered by his experience, and as a result he founded the religion of Aum Shinrikyo in 1987. He called himself "today's Christ" and "the savior of this century."

Asahara was a convincing leader, and the Aum Shinrikyo community spread rapidly in Japan and overseas, with branches in Asia, Europe, and the United States. Eventually, Asahara's largest following outside Japan was in Russia. The disintegration of the Soviet Union and the resulting spiritual chaos had made that region ripe for charismatic spiritual leaders. At a high point, Asahara once preached to more than 15,000 devotees at a Moscow sports stadium.

Yet, as his popularity grew and the cult became more and more prosperous, Asahara became more reclusive and obsessed with danger. A religion once based loosely on Buddhism began to evolve into a hatred for Western society. Asahara claimed the United States had threatened his country and his cult. Edward Sesmond wrote in *Time* that Asahara characterized the United States as a "creature of Freemasons and Jews bent on destroying Japan."

Asahara grew eccentric as he became reclusive. For example, he demanded that his followers always sit one level below him and bow and kiss his big toe in greeting. Having heard something of the cult's day-to-day rituals, a high school classmate of Asahara's told *Time* magazine, "I think Matsumoto is trying to create a closed society like the school for the blind he went to. He is trying to create a society separate from ordinary society in which he can become king of the castle."

Asahara was now a full-fledged charismatic mystic whose claims were as deluded as the practices of his cult were unconventional. He began to see Aum Shinrikyo as its own reality, isolated from the larger world and held above it by his own illusions. He preached that the Japanese government would attempt to wipe out the sect, and that their efforts would coincide with the beginning of the end of the world.

As time passed, Asahara's vision grew darker. In 1995 he wrote a book called *Disaster Approaches the Land of the Rising Sun.* In it, he claimed Armageddon would arrive in a cloud of gas sent from the United States. This event, he

An Aum member, surrounded by photos of leader Shoko Asahara, checks the cult's Web site.

predicted, would happen in either 1997, 1999, or 2000. According to him, survivors would include enlightened followers and 10 percent of the rest of society.

The more unusual the claims Asahara made, the greater his reach became. Aum Shinrikyo experienced a meteoric rise. It recruited heavily at universities, targeting wealthy and educated students who could strengthen the community with cash, which was often obtained from newly initiated members. By 1994 the cult had thirty-six branches and some 10,000 members, as well as many international offices. Some branches served only 100 members and settled for videotaped lectures by Asahara. Russia had six offices and somewhere between 10,000 and 40,000 members.

Yet all was not well with Aum Shinrikyo's community. Members felt pressure from skeptical family and friends outside the Aum community, who accused the cult of psychological manipulation, brainwashing, and brute force. These accusations were based on Aum education practices that included a ban on sexual activity, readings limited to Asahara's writings, self-starvation, immersion in boiling hot or icy cold water, and the repetitive ingestion of drugs.

But what caught the attention of critics was more concrete: One of the provisions of membership called for an inductee to hand over all of his or her property and financial assets to the cult's leaders. One man who eventually left the community revealed that he was asked to hand over his passport and all of his belongings upon joining. After doing so he was forced to work under slave-labor conditions. He later recalled to *Time* magazine, "They promise you heaven, but they make you live in hell."

Still, Asahara enjoyed a position of power and worldwide influence. Even if he was able to operate only on the fringe of society, he was poised to fulfill a dream that lingered deep inside: to inflict a wound on the very society he felt had turned its back on him.

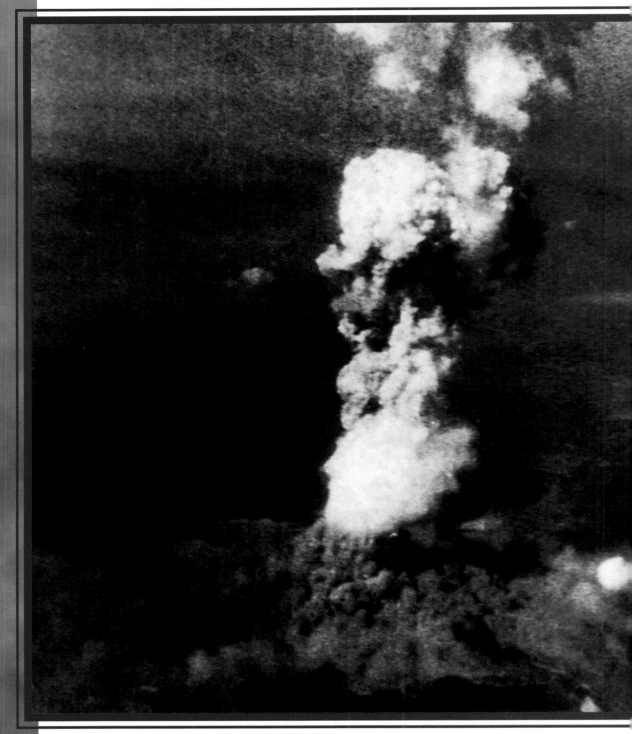

After devastating Japan with two atomic attacks, the United States helped the nation return to economic prosperity in the decades following World War II.

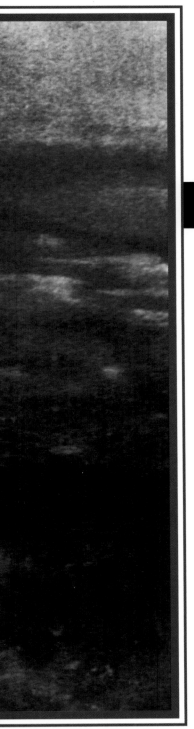

THE SPIRITUAL CLIMATE IN JAPAN

CHAPTER 2

Since the end of World War II (1939–1945) Japan has experienced an ongoing cultural revolution. The horrifying devastation of the atomic bombings of Hiroshima and Nagasaki by the United States sent the country into a state of long-term shock. But by the 1980s, Japan had established itself as a world leader in the manufacture and supply of electronics and automobiles, among other consumer goods. On the coattails of this industrial revolution came prominence in the world market, and in the course of thirty-five years Japan had become Asia's leading representative in the world market.

In 1995, Japan's population was 125.6 million people. Forty-nine percent of the nation's total population lived in the major cities of Tokyo, Osaka, and Nagoya. Tokyo, the nation's capital, boasted some of the most modern offices, hotels, parks, and sports complexes in the world. The economic boom and prosperity of the 1980s continued into the next decade.

The phenomenal rise of a nation that had been brought to its knees at the end of the war is a testament to the character of its people. The Japanese workforce model is a study in dedication, honor, and discipline. Many Western countries divide their workforce into two worlds—one at work, one outside of work. Japan created a model in which home life was incorporated into working life. Factory workers came to work early and stayed late as a point of pride. Activities designed to improve the quality of life, such as exercise and meditation, were brought into the workplace. Working was considered a privilege. Loyalty toward one's employer was the highest priority. Discipline and competence were rewarded. The nation felt it had ground to make up before it reached its potential, and people worked toward that goal as a community rather than as individuals.

By world standards, Tokyo was as clean and safe a city as one could find anywhere. Called the capital city of Asia, Tokyo was an attraction for businesspeople and tourists alike. The Tokyo Exchange was and still is the Wall Street of the Far East. Attractions like Tokyo Disneyland brought in visitors from all over Asia. Yet while commerce and industry

In the latter years of the twentieth century, the high productivity and technological achievement of its workers, along with financial assistance from the United States, made Japan one of the world's strongest economies.

drove the machine, all was not well with the nation's collective spiritual condition.

Religion in Japan

Throughout the course of history, Japan has always been characterized as a country of multiple religions. But in the late nineteenth century, government leaders and nationalistic scholars decided that all religions should exist under a single roof. Thus, the nation was taught to follow a newly created entity, the imperial cult, called State Shinto. The state began to educate the population in the belief that the emperor is a divine descendant of heaven and should be worshipped like a god. From 1868 until the end of World War II, the emperor was the constitutional and absolute leader over the government and the military. But the law of State Shinto that may have had the most significant effect on the culture stated that any superior, be it in the context of government, religion, education, or the workplace, must be obeyed without question.

While not all Japanese believed in the State Shinto, the mandated religion monopolized the country's spiritual and political life. When the Allies abolished the imperial cult after their victory in 1945, the Japanese people were overcome with spiritual confusion. The State Shinto that had until then been held as religious doctrine, and that was part of every aspect of daily life, was suddenly considered dangerous military propaganda. The Allied powers, including the United States, drafted a new constitution and forced the emperor to sign it as part of Japan's surrender agreement. The tenets of the new constitution, effective May 3, 1947, took all governmental power away from the emperor and gave it to the people.

Consequently, a permanent cynicism settled over the nation. This spiritual vacuum that characterized the post-war years in Japan was fertile ground for a wealth of new cults and creeds.

Filling a Spiritual Void

The Japanese have a word that describes a generation of disillusioned youth: *otaku*, a concept that is best translated as an obsession so intense it causes asocial behavior. For these young people, family life almost doesn't exist. Their fathers spend long hours at work, and they are expected to spend much of their spare time at "cram school" or with tutors preparing for the next exam. As a result, a significant minority of children who are raised this way begin to ask serious philosophical questions as they grow into adults. However, because their training has been narrow and goal oriented, they are not equipped to get or find answers. Motivated by an urgent need for meaning, they latch onto any available alternative to their former lives. Some look to yoga and the spiritual enlightenment it promises. Whatever the subject, they immerse themselves in the new interest with great hunger. These circumstances can create a person who is willing, even eager, to throw away his or her life and join a cult.

Aum Shinrikyo followers were trained to do anything for their leader, including break the law. The two Russian members of the cult pictured above stood trial for plotting to blackmail the Japanese government into releasing Shoko Asahara. If the government continued to hold their guru, the men planned on bombing various areas of Japan.

Postwar Japan's spiritual profile was ripe for change. New cults and sects began to pop up on every corner. And while the burst of new religions in Japan can be attributed to the end of the emperor's reign as God, it was encouraged by a new legal system. That system made it easy for almost any individual or group to be officially recognized as a valid religious organization. In addition, religious groups were granted a tax-free status. In 1995, 183,581 religious groups were recognized by the state. Most were considered to be harmless, gentle organizations. Yet there were obvious exceptions.

Aum Shinrikyo was one such cult. Founded in 1987, it combined different aspects of Buddhist and Hindu religions around the practice of yoga. Aum served to fill the spiritual vacuum characteristic of so many Japanese during the economic boom and materialist revolution. It was a time when so many of the nation's youth were either adopting Western values or handing their lives over to unstable, charismatic individuals.

Shoko Asahara's poison-gas attack on the Tokyo subway system landed him on the cover of *Time* magazine. The attack wreaked havoc on the city of eight million, but was not nearly as devastating as Asahara had hoped.

THE SEEDS OF REVENGE

CHAPTER 3

The flourishing of cults in Japan was not regarded as a menace. In fact, quite the contrary was true. In general, these groups were regarded as harmless. Their leaders and their members were considered passive and peaceful.

Yet there were a few exceptions, and Aum Shinrikyo was one of them. As the cult grew in membership and wealth, Shoko Asahara's vision grew darker and more deluded, and his paranoia became more profound. In the end, thousands would suffer. But the gas attack on the Tokyo subway was not the first instance of violence Aum Shinrikyo was responsible for.

Sarin

By the mid 1980s, Asahara had become obsessed with the idea of Armageddon. He began to believe he would play a significant role in bringing about the end of the world. Shortly after the disappearance of attorney Tsutsumi Sakamoto in 1989, Aum Shinrikyo's leaders became fascinated with chemical weapons. The cult's lead scientist, Hideo Murai, was particularly interested in sarin, a gas ten times stronger than cyanide. People exposed to sarin in low doses, such as most of the victims of the Tokyo subway attacks, experience an increased production of saliva, a runny nose, and a feeling that there is pressure exerted on the chest. The eyes' pupils contract, impairing night vision and short-range vision. Other symptoms include slurred speech, headache, and nausea. Victims exposed to higher doses of the chemical suffer difficulty in breathing, coughing, tremors, convulsions, and involuntary discharge of urine and feces. Extremely high doses result in muscular paralysis and the loss of consciousness. These symptoms may develop so rapidly that lesser symptoms do not have time to develop. In these cases, paralysis affects the respiratory center of the central nervous system, causing death by suffocation.

Sarin was developed as an insecticide in the 1930s by a German scientist. The Nazis tested the gas in death camps during World War II and found it could cause significant permanent brain damage. Decades later, Iraqi president

Nazi leaders were interested in using the insecticide sarin in the gas chambers, as seen above, of their death camps. However, they were unable to use it because the compound wasn't perfected until after the end of the war.

Saddam Hussein used the gas against ethnic minorities in Iraq following the Iran-Iraq and Gulf wars.

This fascination with chemical weapons went hand in hand with Asahara's visions of the role he believed he would play in Armageddon. In his preaching, he had begun to mix the traditional teachings of Buddhist salvation, such as compassion and mercy, with images of violence. He demanded that cult members commit violent acts as proof of their devotion to him. Any member who doubted Asahara's vision was tested.

Believing Aum was the world's true savior, members of the cult nearly begged to prove their faith. As one former devotee told an interviewer in Haruki Murakami's book, *Underground,* "[T]hose who did not want to kill people were propelled by faith and, as a result, they killed." Even Asahara was willing to "destroy himself as long as he destroyed as much of the world as possible."

This conditioned obedience and devotion to Asahara drove many cult members to share his vision. Even skeptical followers found themselves willingly contributing to the production of guns, the development of chemical weapons such as anthrax and botulinum, and the acquisition of lasers—weapons of destruction their leader would use in his quest for "salvation." Aum sent representatives to Russia and America to learn how to fly helicopters. The cult even purchased at least one Russian-made MI-17 helicopter. Asahara had planned to use it to spray large amounts of toxic chemicals over urban centers.

But sarin was Asahara's weapon of passion. As his mind deteriorated and he became more and more obsessed with bringing about the end of the world, he became increasingly fixated on sarin. He favored it as a weapon for two primary reasons: First, he felt that the gas, invented in Germany and later used by the Nazis, associated him with his hero, Adolf Hitler. Second, it was efficient. He claimed it was superior because it destroyed people without harming objects, such as buildings.

That Asahara believed he was a guru with superhuman powers wasn't in itself dangerous. Nor was his fixation on sarin. What would prove to be his downfall was his determination to use weapons of mass destruction to bring about the end of the world in order to prove that he would survive it.

Some attention had been attracted by the cult's first attempts to make the chemical sarin. Neighbors of the cult's Mount Fuji compound reported strong odors and dying foliage, the result of a leakage from the sarin labs. But in 1995, a

Police officers raid one of Aum Shinrikyo's many lab buildings in 1999. Years after the subway attacks, Aum was still thought to be developing weapons.

strange event occurred within the compound that drew the suspicion of the police.

In late January, one member of the cult smelled a foul odor. He witnessed some fifty people within the compound immediately become ill. They were coughing, growing dizzy, and passing out. Several members of Aum spent up to three weeks in the hospital, where they were given an antidote to sarin.

The cult immediately issued a press release claiming it had been attacked by outside forces. Asahara believed that he and the cult were being victimized. But many both inside and outside the cult suspected that Asahara had actually ordered the attack on his own people to demonstrate Aum's victimization by the government.

In any case, Asahara used the attack as motivation to develop an even stronger version of sarin. Masami Tsuchiya, Aum's chief chemist, who had learned about the gas in Russia and had manufactured the cult's first usable gas in 1993, was ordered to increase production.

Meanwhile, Asahara laid out his plan. In his confused mind, he justified his actions. First he needed to defend his followers against impending attacks by outside forces. And second, he needed to start World War III to prove he could survive it.

The Attacks

At this time murders within the cult rose dramatically. Members who doubted or questioned cult practices often were brought back in line or killed outright. Asahara appeared to become even more detached from reality. He made claims of glorious past lives, such as one in which he designed and built the oldest of Egypt's Great Pyramids. He had dreams and visions of surviving Hiroshima in a past life. He also had deemed himself above the rules and practices of the cult. While others were forbidden to eat more than the minimal daily allotment of rice and water, he feasted, sometimes eating three dinners in a single evening.

But Asahara's eccentricities were not limited to fantasy and bingeing. He had grown demented in deeper, more profound ways. When it seemed as though Aum would be convicted for the abduction and murder of Kiyoshi Kariya, the notary public whose sister had been swindled out of her building, Asahara grew desperate. Having had some success with a previous experiment with sarin, he decided to use the deadly gas once again.

Several judges in the case against the cult lived with their families in the same neighborhood within the city of Matsumoto. With the verdict some three weeks away, at least one van driving through the neighborhood released a cloud of deadly sarin gas. As a result, seven people were killed and 200 injured. Each of the three judges who lived in the affected area was taken to the hospital for treatment. This was a stunning message to the courts and to the authorities in general. It was also Aum Shinrikyo's first successful attempt on human life outside the cult.

The next attack was to be an attack on Tokyo, a "mini-mass murder." This attack would come before the final attack, which Asahara claimed would serve as the forerunner of Armageddon. (The final attack, of course, never occurred.) Plagued by desperation, paranoia, and megalomania, Asahara ordered Seiichi Endo, a chemist who reported to Murai, to immediately manufacture enough sarin for the job.

Endo had never made sarin before. As a result, the strength of the batch he manufactured was weakened by impurities and would cause far less damage than Asahara had hoped for. But if the guru was aware of the error, he decided impure gas was better than no gas at all. Dizzy with power, he decided to unleash his wave of violence in the Tokyo subways.

Emergency workers in protective suits respond to the sarin attacks on the Tokyo subway system on March 20, 1995.

THE ATTACK ON TOKYO

CHAPTER

O n March 20, 1995, Aum Shinrikyo senior medical doctor Ikuo Hayashi left Aum's local headquarters with his driver, Tomomitsu Nimi. On the way to the subway station, at roughly 7:00 AM, Hayashi stopped at a convenience store to purchase gloves, a knife, tape, sandals, and the daily newspapers.

At 7:48 AM, Hayashi put on a gauze surgical mask—the kind often worn by citizens of Tokyo to prevent the spread of germs—and boarded the front car of the southwest-bound Chiyoda Line, Train A725K. In a newspaper he carried two sealed plastic bags containing liquid sarin. As the train approached Shin-Ochanomizu Station in the central business district,

Hayashi dropped the bags near his right foot and punctured them with the tip of his umbrella, just as he had rehearsed. He quickly walked out of the train and onto the platform. Outside the station he spotted Nimi, and the two of them fled the scene for Aum headquarters as the train continued on.

At 6:00 AM, Kenichi Hirose, a high-level key figure in Aum's Chemical Brigade in the Ministry of Science and Technology, left the cult's local headquarters with his driver, Koichi Kitamura. The pair got in a car and drove to Yotsuya Station, where Hirose boarded the westbound train on the Marunouchi Line. There he changed to a northbound train on the Saikyo Line. He stopped at a station kiosk and purchased a newspaper, in which he wrapped two packets of sarin. He then boarded the second car and stood near the middle.

As the time approached to puncture the bags, Hirose was overwhelmed by a sense of how wrong his actions were. He panicked, and when the train stopped at Korakuen Station he stepped onto the platform. Hirose considered abandoning the mission, but just as he had convinced himself that the horrible results of the act he was about to commit were too much to bear, he regained his composure and boarded the train. "This is nothing less than salvation," Hirose thought, according to Murakami's *Underground*. Besides, he couldn't very well let the others on the mission down. As the train approached Ochanomizu Station, he, like Dr. Hayashi, dropped the bags of sarin near his foot. As the doors opened, he stabbed at the bags with the tip of his umbrella and fled the car.

Japan's subways are known for being extremely crowded, especially during rush hour. Planning the sarin attack for the morning commute allowed the Aum Shinrikyo cult to affect a large number of people. Some 5 million commuters use Japan's subways each day.

Kiyotaka Tonozaki drove Masato Yokoyama, an Aum physicist, toward the Shinjuku Station. Like the others, they stopped to buy a newspaper to wrap the sarin packets in. Yokoyama donned a wig and fake glasses, then boarded the Marunouchi Line train bound for Ikebukuro. He sat in the fifth car from the front. As the train pulled into Yotsuya Station, he dropped the bags and poked them with the tip of his umbrella. Remarkably, only one packet was punctured, and only once. The other lay harmlessly on the floor of the car. As the train stopped, he stepped onto the platform and located Tonozaki, who drove him back to the local Aum headquarters.

Identical packets containing 900 milliliters of sarin were dropped and punctured at two more stations on the Tokyo Metropolitan Subway. Toru Toyoda punctured both of his bags and released all the sarin on a northeast-bound Hibiya Line train as it approached Ebisu Station. As a test of devotion, Yasuo Hayashi was given three packets of sarin. He boarded the third car of the A720S train from Kita-senju at Ueno. When the train reached Akihabara, he punctured the bags.

As Yasuo Hayashi left the Chiyoda Line train, the liquid sarin ran out on the floor and began to evaporate. Passengers showed symptoms of poisoning immediately. They coughed, slurred their words, and collapsed in the car and on the platform. Hundreds suffered serious effects. Two station attendants attempting to remove the bags did not survive. Pandemonium and confusion reigned. No one was quite sure what was happening. Those who could move fled. Some stepped over the fallen victims. Others stopped to help carry the sick out of the station into the fresh air. The train was stopped and evacuated at the next station. Unbeknownst to all, this was only the beginning.

After exiting the train at Ochanomizu Station, Kenichi Hirose found Koichi Kitamura's car. He rinsed the tip of the umbrella with bottled water and placed it in the trunk. But despite his care, he began to display the symptoms of sarin poisoning. He had difficulty breathing and could not speak. He injected himself in the thigh with a syringe full of atropine sulphate, a sarin antidote given to him by Ikuo Hayashi.

Asahara had instructed the attackers to go to specific hospitals after releasing the sarin. There, Aum doctors would give them a foolproof sarin antidote. As planned, Kitamura drove the car to the hospital. He was surprised to find that the doctors there were unaware of the surefire antidote Asahara had promised. The two returned to local headquarters, where Hirose was treated by Dr. Hayashi.

Back at Nakano-Sakaue Station, the most severe casualties were taken above ground. One later

Rescuers paid a price for their quick arrival on the scene of the sarin gas attacks: Most of those injured were government workers and station attendants.

died. As the train continued on its route, passengers complained of illness. Several attendants were rushed to the hospital, where they were treated for poisoning.

Similar reports came from the other three train lines. Large numbers of casualties were cleared off of the Hibiya Line train, yet the car continued to Shinjuku Station, then was sent back in the other direction as normal. An hour and forty minutes after the sarin was spilled, the train was finally stopped and

While many subway riders ran for their lives during the gas attacks, some remained to assist stricken passengers.

evacuated. Altogether, twelve people died and more than 5,000 were treated for injuries. The majority of the victims by far were government employees and station attendants.

Aum Shinrikyo's attack, believed to have been masterminded by Hideo Murai, was choreographed perfectly and executed with precision. All but two of the eleven sarin packets had been punctured, releasing the toxic gas into the confined spaces of the subway cars and the underground stations. The plan called for the gas to be released between 8:09 AM and 8:13 AM, just as workers were arriving at their destinations to begin the workday.

If there was a saving grace, it was that the sarin was a "bad" batch. The truth is that casualties could have been far greater. At full strength, just a drop of sarin is enough to kill. In smaller amounts it can cause permanent brain damage. Still, the effects were significant.

Those who suffered direct contact with the toxin were not alone in feeling the effects of the attack. Televised scenes of police in full protective gear filled Japan's homes. Television also brought footage of stricken commuters splayed on sidewalks, their heads propped back and blood running from their mouths. Countless others were shown doubled over and coughing. Shoko Asahara's ultimate act of violence had succeeded not because it wounded thousands. It had reached millions, striking terror into a nation that considered itself above such brutal acts of violence.

Members of Japan's military comb through a subway car seeking evidence and cleaning up after the sarin attacks.

THE COUNTERATTACKS

While hundreds of thousands of dazed commuters evacuated the subway stations where the gas attacks occurred, thousands of other people became heroes. Police, subway employees, and common citizens rushed to the aid of the victims. These brave individuals offered first aid, cold compresses, and words of encouragement. They helped victims out of the stations. The also monitored the ill until emergency personnel arrived to administer medical care.

These heroes came from all walks of life, including one, a driver for a local television news station, who found himself in the unlikely role of ambulance driver. Minoru Miyata, who was fifty-four at the time, had served as a TV Tokyo chauffeur for six years. His job entails long periods of time on standby until a news story breaks, when he drives a van full of broadcasting equipment to the scene.

March 20 found Miyata driving leisurely to a location to film stock footage for a program. When he reached the financial district, he was struck by the confusion surrounding the busy intersection. At that moment, a call came over the radio directing him to the Kasumigaseki crossing, a large plaza near the Ministries of Foreign Affairs, Finance, and Trade and Industry, among others. There he saw four subway workers in their green uniforms. Some were kneeling and others were stretched out on the sidewalk. A young man was shouting for an ambulance. As time was of the essence, Miyata offered to take them to the hospital in the TV van. He and his colleagues unloaded the equipment and laid two subway attendants across the back seat. A third joined Miyata in the front.

One of the victims was Assistant Stationmaster Takahashi, perhaps the best known of the victims. Takahashi had just been relieved of his shift when the car carrying the sarin pulled into the station. He volunteered to clean up the oily liquid, having no idea it would kill him.

Miyata and the van reached Hibiya Hospital in a matter of minutes, but the doctors and nurses had not yet heard of the attacks. They kept the group waiting for more than an hour before admitting them. By then Takahasi was too sick to save. He died later that day. Miyata describes the morning in no uncertain terms in *Underground*: "When you've worked as long as I have, you get to see all kinds of scenes. I even went to the Kobe earthquake. But the Tokyo gas attack was different. That was really and truly hell."

The Response

Although Tokyo was caught off guard by the attacks, the police's response was well-planned. City officials rushed to man parks and other public places with hundreds of armed guards. While rumors circulated through the city, police drew up a list of suspects. Within days the Japanese government launched a full-fledged attack on Aum Shinrikyo.

The counterassault involved 2,500 heavily armed troops, who stormed twenty-five Aum facilities across Japan. Some wore protective suits with gas detectors. Others carried caged canaries, which were watched closely: If a bird died, there was sure to be lethal gas in the air. But there was no deadly gas to speak of. Cult members appeared to know the police were coming. As police approached the primary compound at Kamikuishiki, 110 miles west of Tokyo, Aum devotees flooded the grounds with searchlights. The police reached a makeshift barricade near the entrance, where they heard a man shouting, "The Aum Supreme Truth has nothing to hide. It is an unjust search, but we will cooperate."

Members of the media converge upon the headquarters of Aum Shinrikyo as Japanese police officials search the compound for evidence in the gas attacks.

Upon entering the compound, the siege party found shocking living conditions. Inside were fifty tiny cubicles, each just large enough to accommodate a single cult member lying on a blanket. Everyone appeared to be suffering from malnutrition, though they claimed they were fasting voluntarily. Six Aum members were hospitalized, but the only arrests included doctors on the grounds and a single cult official.

In a nearby warehouse investigators discovered large quantities of toxic chemicals, including the basic ingredients used in the manufacture of sarin. Cult spokesmen claimed the chemicals were for making pottery and semiconductors for cult-owned businesses. This seemed unlikely. The large volume of chemicals indicated that the place was operating as a lab or factory.

Similar stockpiles were found in other offices and warehouses. All told, raiding parties uncovered tons of chemicals, including sodium cyanide, sodium fluoride, phosphorus trichloride, and acetonitrile. One newspaper guessed that there were enough chemicals to kill 4.2 million people. Another estimated 10 million people. As Japanese television viewers watched, police combed through the property, seeking clues that would lead to the discovery of the party responsible for the twelve deaths and countless injuries. The following Thursday, police declared for the first time their intention of bringing in the cult's guru, Shoko Asahara, for questioning on the attacks in the Tokyo subway.

The Guru Denies Involvement

Meanwhile, Asahara lay in hiding. He was protected by a band of handpicked supporters that he trusted to keep his location secret. Aum lawyers declared outrage at the raids. Asahara secretly released two radio broadcasts. In one, intended for the public, he pleaded, "I am innocent," over and over in a singsong voice. He denied involvement in Kiyoshi Kariya's kidnapping. He also denied harmful intentions for the chemical stockpile. "I don't understand," he said, "why it's said that these can be used to make sarin."

In a separate video, intended for his followers and broadcast at thirty-six local Aum chapters, Asahara claimed Aum had been the target of a poison gas attack. Once again, he declared the United States responsible. "Disciples," he proclaimed, "the time to awaken and help me is upon you. Let's carry out the salvation plan and face death without regrets."

The fact that the guru created conflicting messages for audiences of distinctly different interests seemed to confirm his guilt. It also betrayed his unraveling mental state. Yoshinobu Aoyama, Asahara's lawyer, made the following public announcement: "We practice our religion on the basis of Buddhist doctrines such as no killing, so it is impossible that we are responsible. In my personal view, sarin could not be made by those other than special persons like those in the U.S. military. I speculate that someone in the military and state authorities may have been involved." He then called the police raids "unprecedented religious persecution."

Meanwhile, authorities intensified the investigation of the cult. They addressed more than 100 complaints and tested soil outside the Kamikuishiki warehouses and offices. Over the following weeks police arrested more than 150 cult members. Many of the raids and arrests were televised. All of Japan was mesmerized by the drama as authorities took small but certain steps to capture the cult leadership.

In a bizarre twist to an already freakish manhunt, Hideo Murai, thought to be the mastermind of the subway attack, was stabbed to death in front of TV cameras and ten police officers. The nation watched Hideo Murai clutch his abdomen as he knelt in a pool of blood, a dazed look on his face. Some claim that Asahara had ordered the attack so that Murai could not testify against him.

Holding a banner depicting Shoko Asahara, a demonstrator protests the re-emergence of Aum Shinrikyo. Although the cult was found responsible for the gassing of the Tokyo subway system, it was nevertheless still allowed to operate throughout Japan.

Still, Asahara remained at large. "We used to believe that Japan was a safe country," Kazuko Koyama, a Tokyo office clerk, told *Newsweek* magazine. "I am not so sure if it's true anymore." This would turn out to be a gross understatement. A manhunt, arrest, and still more dramatic events were on the horizon.

People throughout Japan were relieved when Shoko Asahara, in the back-seat of a car *(above)*, was taken into custody two months after the attacks.